THE POETRY BOOK

Volume 1

Am I Falling

By: Esther Litchfield-Fink

Table of Contents

Chapter 1
Am I Falling

So I Wanna Be Perfect
I'm Doing Nothing Today
Failure
Muse, Muse, Where Are You
I Forgot It Was Tuesday
Why Didn't He Want Me
I Could Wander
When You're Happy and you Know It

So I Wanna Be Perfect

so I wanna be perfect
but not today
because it's already tonight
and the moon is staring at me
thru slats in the shades
as if to say
i see you.

so i wanna be perfect
but not today
because i already did
so many things
imperfectly
that i cannot fix
today.

so i wanna be perfect
but not today
because who am i kidding
really
i just had cake before bed

and perfect people don't do that
especially with icing and sprinkles
because they know better
so they do better
but not me.

so i wanna be perfect
but not today
because the only thing left
to do
when it's almost midnight
is pray
but that feels like a cop out
because He loves me anyway.

so i wanna be perfect
just like the lady
on the screen in my hand
with her soft voice
and her story
of her successful day
and how i could do it too
if i just follow her
life
day by day.

and there's a handsome young guy
passing by

in the background
in her large clean kitchen
that has large windows
cooking them lunch
wearing an apron
and a smirk
that does it
really.

so i wanna be perfect
and reach all my goals
and go down my lists
and check all the boxes
while smiling and cooking
and shopping and working
and building up muscle
while slimming and thinning
and walking
the highest of wires
of life
doing my art
with no safety net
with children to feed
with rain on the roof
yet
responsibilities
keep me from doing it all
perfectly. or so i think?

so i wanna be perfect
but not today
i tire of thinking
and planning
and scheming
of how my life
will turn out to be
when i get it all
together
perfectly
what happens then?

Humpty Dumpty
fell off the wall
eventually.
and so will i
once i get it together
so perfectly.

so what is the point
of all the frustration
to climb up the wall
to all that perfection
if just to sit for second or two
all put together
for that pic? or two.
for we all fall

down
eventually
and you know how the poem ends
even kids know.
how all the kings horses
and all the kings men
are left scrambling for perfection
never to have it again.

I'm Doing Nothing Today

i'm doing nothing today
too bad on you
you think you could call me
and tell me what to do
well you can because you pay me to

i'm doing nothing today
too bad on you
you can tell me what to do
but i can ignore you
because i want to
and need to
rest my weary brain

i'm doing nothing today
too bad on you
take your carrot on a stick
my paycheck my day check
my i don't wanna work check
and toss it in the river
that i'll be sitting at

waiting for the fish
to chew on the worm
at the end of my stick
in the sun

i'm doing nothing today
too bad on you
there's cereal and milk
and cans of things
and drinks and snacks
and bread and jars
of peanuts ground
for days like this
when i wanna do nothing
so figure it out little people
figure it out
after you don't make your beds.

i'm doing nothing today
too bad on you
i need new clothes
to look good in
while doing nothing
so off to the store
to sort through the racks
shirt by shirt
shoe by shoe
and fill my cart

cz i have nothing to do
but look cool
while i do nothing today

i'm doing nothing today
too bad on you
i'll climb up the mountain
i always wanted to
and sit at the top
and eat food
in my backpack
while seeing the view.

i'm doing nothing today
too bad on you
as i pass by the piano
i'll wipe dust off the keys
and play a song or two
or three or four
and get lost in the music
created by those
that flipped off their paychecks
and day-checks and said
woe is you i'm not working
i'm shirking the day-check and paycheck
to write songs
so we could all sing
while we work

and stay sane
in this maze and haze
called the world
and so i play and play.

i'm doing nothing today
too bad on you
i'm talking to no one
i'm doing nothing
i'm being no one
to no one

all while wearing new clothes
and fishing for fish
and looking at views
from mountains so high
and playing the songs
that i'm here to play
while i'm doing nothing
it's too bad on you

have a good day.
I did.

Failure

at last
failure.
you hated that place
that space
that waste
of time

at last
failure.
they pushed you
and pulled you
and told you
and scolded
your ways
and your days
when you really did good

at last
failure.
you tried and you cried
you died you survived

thinking you're wrong all along.
you're a star and a song
that performs with grace
in your place
in your space
and for that you're disgraced.

at last
failure.
for being good
for doing good
just
as you should.

while you walk out the door
they stay in the hood
with their noses held high
and the sky
is the limit for you.
while they fumble and bumble
you trip and fall
as you're pushed out the door
and then-
you realize
with surprise
that you've been set free.

at last.
failure set you free.

only,
you know that there was no fail you prevailed
and made it to the end
they failed to see
you.
go free
and look
and see
how free you are
failure was to stay
and now you're free.
who cares who thinks
you failed.
that is your get-out-of-jail-card.
poor you, they think
and you're on the brink
of the best that's yet to come.

Muse, Muse, Where Are You

muse, oh muse.
where are you
sometimes i feel like
you want a kidney.
i mean how fair is that?
all i ask
is that you appear
to be near
and enter my heart
and soul
and spirit
at the exact moment I want you
to help me create
when i'm not washing dishes
or doing laundry
or cooking
or sweeping
or sleeping
or swiping
or working for a paycheck
so i'm not homeless.

muse, oh muse.
where are you
a kidney. really?
that's what you want?
can i coax you
and tempt you
with whispers so soft
of secrets and stories
of passions and glory
stories with heroes
i mean heroines
ok both.

muse, oh muse.
where are you
where hide you
where sleep you
when i need you
when i want you
when i make time
finally

my place at my desk
with my fingers
poised
ready for magic
that i will create
when you come

visit with me.
when i sit
and i'm ready
to greet you.
and meet you
i'll close my eyes
so you
breathe into me
creativity.

muse, oh muse.
where are you
you tease me
and taunt me
and haunt me
i know you're there
somewhere
waiting to land
but you won't on command.
do you laugh as i stumble
and bumble
to form the right art
from my heart
do you see me start
and stop and
stamp my foot
throw the lamp
slam

cry
sigh
and beg. and i almost never beg.
 i'm not the type.

i'm ready and waiting
and you ghost me.

muse, oh muse.
where are you
you ghost
when i need you the most.
my days work is done
and i wait
for my fate
to turn
with my next creation
that fame and elation
i seek
i yearn for
when you meet me
i meet you
we make love
-ly things together
stabbed in the heart
i sit alone
in front of another blank page.

muse, oh muse.
where are you
guess what.
who cares
i'm done with you
you're worthless
you're banished
don't bother calling
i'm going to bed.
and forget your ruse
your notion
of devotion
you pour upon me
while i sleep
or drive
or swim
or walk outside
to try to forget you.
i know your tricks very well
the spell
you cast
when at last
you come
but i haven't got a pencil
or a red light
or a dry hand
or a place
to place

the thoughts that come
flooding
the dam that breaks
and the rush of ideas
that flow
when i know
i can't catch them
ever again.

muse, oh muse.
maybe one day
we will meet again
at the same time and place
and then
it will be rainbows
and unicorns
coming together
to create some magic
that never existed before.
until then
my kidney is mine.

I Forgot It Was Tuesday

i forgot it was Tuesday
and that's a problem
not because i wonder
if my memory has gone
but the significance
of hearing the garbage truck
outside my window.
and what luck
i forgot
to pull my garbage cans
to the curb
again.

i forgot it was Tuesday
and that's a problem
because all my neighbors
have it together
with their neat garbage cans
lined up at the end
of their driveways
and to boot

their cans have covers.
not mine.
i forgot it was Tuesday
and that's a problem
because i have enough
on my brain
i don't need more garbage
piling up
and blocking all my good thoughts
and plans
because all i can think of
is what kind of person
forgets
to do a simple thing
like pull a can of garbage
to the curb
on time.

i forgot it was Tuesday
and that's a problem
because now i have to wait
until Friday
when i can put the garbage out
and then i can begin
to think clearly
once again.
that's three days away.

i forgot it was Tuesday
and that's a problem
because the loud sound
of the truck
pulling away
without my garbage
is like a song that plays
over and over
inside your head
and refuses to leave.

how do you get a song
out of your head
when it's lodged inside
and seems to hide
not letting in
any new thoughts.

all because i forgot
that it was Tuesday
and that's a problem
because here's the thing
i'm trying to be perfect
and it's not working very well.
Instead
I dwell
on how
I fell

apart
all because
I forgot
a
simple
task.

maybe I forgot it was Tuesday
because
i was studying
and working
and writing
a best seller
cooking and caring
for children
that will grow up to be
all kinds of great things
i never got to be
maybe i was busy
playing the piano.
you see
i learned to play a new song
on the piano
in anticipation and
preparation
so i could play it when the garbage
of life
in my head

overflows
and the piano
calms me down
when
i forget things like Tuesday.

i forgot it was Tuesday
and that's a problem
for it's the day
that i gauge
how i'm doing
in life.
when i remember
that Tuesday is garbage day
that sets the tone for the week
to see if i'm a-ok
or a big mess
of a person
that will never succeed.
at anything.
everything
rides on
the garbage
at the curb on time
and the sound of the truck
and if it's carrying away
my thoughts
or leaving them behind

for me
to keep
turning and churning
it all in my mind
until next Tuesday
when i get a re-do on life
thank God for redoes.
i don't have to live like this
forever.
there is always another
Tuesday.

Why Didn't He Want Me?

why didn't he want me
i mean i'm nice
a little too nice?
why didn't he want me
i mean i'm smart
but not smarter than him
which is good.
why didn't he want me
i mean i'm a lot of things
that make people want me
like pretty and a little bit funny
but not too funny
and i'm tall
but not too tall
the perfect amount of tall

why didn't he want me
i can't think it up
it could be anything
or maybe it's that one thing

that i just can't think of
that must be it.

that one thing
that made him not want me
to be his anything
even his biggest fan
but maybe he didn't want a fan
so that can't be it
that one thing
that i don't know what it is
so why didn't he want me.

why didn't he want me
after he said he did
and i said i did.
i know my hands were warm enough
i know my lips were soft enough
i know my dress was nice enough
but i wasn't enough.
maybe that's it
that's the one thing.
it was me.

I Could Wander

i could wander alone
i could hike
i could roam
camp out in a cabin
a beach or a tree

i could wander alone
eat meals on my own
berries and nuts
and drink from the stream
like Thoreau

i could wander alone
no need for a home
think thoughts
and write books
and be happy
and free

oh i forgot
i can't wander alone

for how would my little and big ones succeed?
oh i forgot

i can't wander or roam
there are people to feed
and a roof to repair
and beds to be made
and clothes to be had
and hair to be brushed
and papers to sign
and teachers to please
and scraped knees to keep clean
and alarm clocks to set
and lights to turn out
and bedtimes and mealtimes and fun times
and done times and
oh i forgot

i can't wander or roam
there are kisses to give
and laughter to share
and bruises to soothe
and lives to be planned
oh i forgot

i can't wander or roam
thoughts must be stolen
and poems written

when no one is needing
or heeding
or looking
for me to give kisses
or soup in clean dishes
woods that have cabins
are dreams in my head
when i go to bed
and dream of the day
i could wander and roam
which may never be
i can see
that the dream
is a dream
is a dream
i could have in my mind
again and again
and again
and again
and again and again and again.

When You're Happy And You Know It

when you're happy and you know it
don't you show it
if you do
you're screwed
by all those lovelies

when you're happy and you know it
don't you show it
it's not the ones
that hate
or berate
or have distaste
for you
that want you sad
and mad
and bad

when you're happy and you know it
don't you show it
to your friends or your sis
to your bro

or those
that "mean well"
or hell
will break loose
as they don't know how
to hold you
with your joy

when you're happy and you know it
don't you show it
even though you want to.
send your vibes to the sky
or write them in sand
or swim them in the sea
those happy, happy vibes
that flow
from you
dance their dance just you
and
your happiness
until it leaves
and your bro and your sis
your neighbor
and friend
can once again
hold you in your pain
and stroke your hair
there there.

we're here for you
now.

when you're happy and you know it
don't you show it
keep your happy
close to your heart.
if happy came to you
then it's yours.

Chapter 2
I'm Not Shouting

Shine Too Bright
I Wanna Glow Up
Things Unsaid
You Showed Me A Sign
But I Paid You A Dollar
I'll Be A Little Late

Shine Too Bright

shine too bright
shine too bright
you shine too bright
you see.

they sit in dark
they can't be still
they spin so fast
inside their heads
it's dark
they spin
they cannot see
you.

or your light.
or your bright.
or your still.

you shine too bright
shine too bright

you blind them
can't you see

they blame you
shame you
shoot you
down
to darken you like them
you see

run away. run my friend
run away with me.
to only be
with those
who truly want to see.

it may be only you and me
that want to shine you see
we'll shine so bright
and share the light
just you, just you and me.
so shall it be.
Maybe.

I Wanna Glow Up

what's a glow up
I ask my kid
she rolls her eyes
and starts to scroll
and there on her screen
she points out to me
how easy it can be
to turn into anyone
you wanna be.
oh. it's that easy,
one tick one tock
you're glowed up.

what's a glow up
I type in the search
frantically.
I don't want to miss out
and fall behind
and be the one
that fails yet another trend
so I pretend
that I know what's going on
that i'm in with the in crowd
the glowed up crowd

because I think i've been glowing down
if that's even a thing.
I mean it is for me.

what's a glow up
I know who could help
who won't roll her eyes at me
it's Siri.
I ask, she tells.
whoa that's a lot
of
"here's what I found on the web"
well i'm a good student
so off to the races I go.
sucked in by the lure
of glamor and shine
hairstyles, makeup
shopping and workouts
see how she did it
before and after

so out comes my pen
and then
I write it all down
the stuff I must buy now

blushes and brushes
eyelashes, glosses
and
glue.

glue! I don't dare ask
what i'm gluing where
for
if I dare
I may have to remain
looking like I do
when I wake up.

that's not allowed
you don't want to glow down.
the whole point I see
is to
look like someone new.
different than you are
like a star
walking down the boulevard.

I put my pen down.
wait -
I don't walk down boulevards
I don't ride in fancy cars
I mean I want to
but what comes first
the car or the star
do I need the lashes
to reach the status
so I can show up
glowed up
with the glowed up people?
oh. no.

i'm all mixed up.

I don't know what to do
"Siri, are you there?"
help. don't you care?
glow up, glow up
I need to glow up

donut? she says
are you looking for donuts?

G LO W E D   U P

I say really slow.
oh.
"so here's what I found in the web for donuts"
I take out my pen
once again
and write what she says
so I can follow her lead
and do what I know
which is to go buy donuts
to go eat donuts.

she gets me that Siri. she gets me.

Things Unsaid

things unsaid
where do they go?
I don't know where yours go
or maybe you don't have any
maybe you speak your mind
well i'm not that kind.
I only speak my mind
when i'm sure
that
the words that leave my brain
and my heart
have a safe place to land
and call home with no chance of
disdain or pain
or worse.
laughter or
rejection.

things unsaid
where do they go?
mine take walks inside my brain
they flutter in my gut

and grab on to my heart
and don't want to part
but sometimes they make it out.

things unsaid
where do they go?
the ones that escape, I mean
those words that make it out
and land in the little yellow notepad
on my phone
so I could tell them to you
when the perfect moment arrives

things unsaid
where do they go?
they get told to other people
because it's too scary
to
say it straight to your face
and those other people
alway say
the same thing -

'tell him! tell him!'

and I don't.
because I mean,
easy for them to say
they're not the one that

like likes you.
ok loves you.
see there I go again
telling all these other people
readers of my poems
that I don't even know
that I like like you.

things unsaid
where do they go?
to the wrong places
to the wrong people
whats if the world ends
and I never got to see your face
when I tell you something I hate about you
when I tell you something I love about you
when I tell you all the things unsaid
now that i'm thinking about it
the dread
is leaving them unsaid.

so here goes
I hate you
and I love you.
there.
it's said.

You Showed Me A Sign

last time i saw you
you showed me a sign
that you thought i was fine
like 'she's gonna be mine'
for a night anyway

last time i saw you
you looked mighty fine
yourself,
i would say
i could play
with you for a day
or more

last time i saw you
you showed me a sign
more than one i would say
that you wanted to play
with me for a day or a night
or a week or a year or so

last time i saw you
my wheels started spinning
my heart started thumping
as you were reaching and showing me
just how you wanted to play

last time i saw you
i took it all in
your grin
your charm
your muscles and biceps
and thigh-cepts and triceps
and all of that fine looking form
that is you

last time i saw you
i had a nice time
and i left before anything
got out of hand
i tossed and i turned
for days upon days
and nights were so fine
and sublime
full of thoughts of us meeting again

next time i saw you
i readied myself
for the rumble and tumble

and fumble that comes
when he thinks you're fine
and sublime and divine

next time i saw you
i came with all bells
and all whistles and colors
and scents like the flower bed
out in the park
a skip in my step
and a thing in my heart
for a start
of some talks and walks and more

next time i saw you
you said please and thank you
and offered me tea and a
how do you do
where was the rest?
the best i remembered
where you were so savage
ripping apart
my heart,
my dreams for a start
of something so fun
that could run for days
or nights or both
for a while

next time i saw you
i left with a dread
that the first time i saw you
was all in my head
the pleasure turned pain
and i felt your disdain
in your lack of attention
to what i was thinking
and dreaming
and hoping
would be
last time i saw you
you showed me no sign
was it mine?
that i made up
in my head?
did i say something do something
make a mistake?
so what happens now?
do i hide out and see
that it was all me
or do i try one more time
to look for a sign
that you thought i was fine
like 'she's gonna be mine'
or do i tally it off as i cry and i die
of my own silly lie
that he thought i was fine

and divine
maybe it was just me
you see
maybe i'll never know.
until next time.

But I Paid You A Dollar

do the work do the work
i paid you a dollar
be happy be happy
i paid you a dollar

do the work do the work
i paid you a dollar
stop living
stop loving
stop driving
stop sleeping
i paid you a dollar
to work for me

where are you
where are you
i paid you a dollar
work harder
work longer
i paid you a dollar
a dollar? i ask?

a dollar! says he
don't worry
don't worry
more dollars will come
i don't want your dollar
or the one that will come
yet I do need your dollar
those dollars they suck
they get passed around
to keeping us alive

do the work do the work
i paid you a dollar
NO say i

i'll drink from the river
and eat from the sea
i'll sleep in the woods
peacefully.
keep your dollar.

I'll Be A Little Late

i'll be a little late
is that ok
he says via text
followed by a cute emoji
thinking it will help
it doesn't.

i'll be a little late
is that ok
with no question mark
like it's already ok with him
so of course it's ok
with me.
are you kidding?
i have a call
and a job
the bank closes at 3
the post office at 4
my dr's at 2
what happens
when you're late?

the dominos fall
don't you know what
happens
to dominoes?
buddy here's a lesson
one taps the next
and the next
and the rest
fall neatly in a row
flat on their faces
the races
of the day are over
lost before they began
my plan
to dominate the day
i watch as my life
falls
apart.

i'll be a little late
is that ok
no it's not
the scent of cinnamon spice
sprinkled on foil
to make the place smell fake nice
will disappear
by the time you get here.
the dog will wake up

his perfectly timed meal
will now need to appear
when you're here
and then all you'll do
is play with Spot
and i'll be toast. burnt toast.
on the sidelines
of the delay
in your day.

i'll be a little late
is that ok
my lipstick smear
will have disappeared
like the joy in my heart
fading
away
as i watch as the day
takes a life of its' own
and so i say
it's ok
be late
i'll wait
in another place
where i have to be
to see
that my date is with me
i now have time

for that walk outside
to breathe in
the fresh air
without a care
for the hour i thought
was wasted
away
but hey
i found it to be
for me.

Chapter 3
Icing On a Cake

Enemies
To My Gurus
Black and White Body

Enemies

keep 'em close keep 'em close
and watch what they do
pretend you like 'em
say you care
so they don't dare
betray you

keep 'em close keep 'em closer
and watch what they say
pretend you hear
pretend you care
so they don't dare
destroy you

keep 'em close
so close
so close
so you can barely breathe
and watch how their walls
come down
come down

until you're no longer
their clown

keep 'em close
keep 'em close
and hope they almost die
while you live your life
on top of the world
you built when they destroyed you.

let them drift
let them drift
thinking they're safe
and they won the war with you
let them drift
let them drift
thinking what they may
while you smile and live
while you laugh and dance
while you hug and kiss
and forget to diss
cz you built your place
drawbridge in place
keeping only the good ones inside your space.
and they drift. away. from you.

To My Gurus

to my gurus
you know who you are
rabbis and preachers
buddhists and teachers
that come from all places
all over the world

to teach me
to heal me
reveal me to me
on podcasts
on mountains
in places and spaces
that show me the graces
of what can be done
and won
when seeking with faith
and with pain
from heartbreak
and sorrow
not wanting to see

today or tomorrow
anymore

to my gurus
you know who you are
did i find you
or did you find me
in places of prayer
in hot rooms in cold
in whispers and hints
some loud and some bold

without you all
i would have disappeared
into thin air
like a wisp of a thought
a passing breeze
that ruffles no feathers
stays out of bad weather
hides from the storms of life
and never gets to see
how good it can be
to live and believe
be strong and succeed
at finding myself
amidst shame and regret
and to never forget
that all the roads

you all led me to
lead to myself
inside
where god resides
with peace and pride
for life on this earth
which is actually quite fun.

Black and White Body

I run my fingers up
I run my fingers down
softly, slowly,
up and down
faster, harder
louder still
pressing down
with the bottom
of my foot
up and down
as well.

I run my fingers up
I run my fingers down
I close my eyes
and listen
and forget about the world
because it doesn't exist
when i'm playing you
black and white
I hear you

hear my cry
my sigh
you mimic me
and create sounds of your own
to drown out
everything
and leave the sound
of the ticking
metronome
harmonize
and vaporize
the unnecessary
which is everything
except you.

I run my fingers up
I run my fingers down
and create a sound
that teases
that pleases
upbeat downbeat
all around beat
sounding off
depending where I touch you
you soothe me as I soothe you
my lover and friend
you tell me your stories
and i'll tell you mine

do we have a deal?
of course we do
there is no joy in the world like you
you will never betray me
although I sometimes disappear
for a while
trying to live in the world
but I always come back to your
cool-to-the-touch body
i'm drawn
you're magnetic
you make me happy
maybe this is true love
how lucky am I
that you came into my life
as a gift
long ago
you're still here
and so am I

lets make music forever
together.
you speak to me when words fail.
my piano. my one true love.

Chapter 4
Much Ado About Love

The Pandemic in my Heart
Oh So Many Boys I Love
Another Book Arrived in the Mail
Back to the Place

The Pandemic In My Heart

people around
are busy about
the plague
and the state of the world

people around
are doing their part
in filling their places
and houses and spaces

people around
are sitting and standing
and pacing and tracing
and eating and sleeping

but me i just sit
with my hand on my heart
and wonder
and ponder
and worry
about where you are

but me i just stand
or lay all day
and stare at the ceiling
still holding my heart

while people around
are thinking and drinking
and planning and dealing
and feeling and screaming
and fighting for their lives.

but me i just lay
and trace tears on my face
i know not where you stand
or what you do
or what you want

but me i just think
and pretend of a world
where play was ok
and you'd be here today
and people around
would sing out our song
and along would be peace
in the world.

Oh So Many Boys I Love

oh so many boys I love
let's start with Freddie
how could I not
his style and his smile
his rhapsodies just capture me
and into love I fall
his crown and royal garb he wears
while singing playing, fooling around
Bohemian man! flamboyant man! you make me
think
I too,
can
do anything.

oh so many boys I love
don't mind, Freddie
but Chris is also the man
he makes the sun rise
over Jordan
in Yellow
like magic

and when he smiles like a kid
I think I can be a kid too.

playing his riff on the piano
makes all the clocks STOP
like my heart
for the sweet and hot Chris

oh so many boys I love
move over Chris
the jazz man John cometh
voice solemn and fine
like wine
on a dinner table
smooth and a little nasty
rough around the edges
in conversation
and likely other things
just ask Taylor
wait you don't have to ask her
she told us all about it, John dear
we know your'e not the kindest soul on the planet
but boy your musics' got soul
and for that I love, love, love you.

to be continued...there are so many of you.

Another Book Arrived in the Mail

another book
arrived in the mail
I knew it was a book
from the look
and feel
of the brown wrapped paper
white label
slapped on
with my name
and my address
it was for me

another book
arrived in the mail
was it my textbook
for college?
or the romance reader
with the guy
that has naked abs
and long flowing hair
on the cover?

ha ha lol that was a joke
I don't read books
with blokes
that bring me pleasure
ever.

another book
arrived in the mail
could be that workbook
that matches the rulebook
of how to be grateful
in this day and age
so life won't fall apart.

another book
arrived in the mail
maybe the one
with the story and glory
of how one great star
started out poor and small
and ended up high
on the mountain of life.
I could use that right about
now.

another book
arrived in the mail
the new one by Greene

that probes into psyches
and minds of the humans
and secrets and plans
are revealed to be used
and abused until
you get what you want
and win. and I want to win.
not sure what the prize is though.

my eyes cannot focus
my head starts to spin
what world am I in
the stories collide
inside my mind
I put one back on the shelf
remove another
frantically searching
for answers to my troubles
that books are supposed to solve.

I toss them
I shelve them
my fingers are cold
i'm hungry
and truth be told
when did I eat
or sleep last?
with all these stories

of people
with glory
and gory
lives
and bad lives
and made up lives
and outlines
of helping the self
of running away
of today
tomorrow
and yesterday

I fall on the floor
surrounded
by tales
of old
before books were even printed
but written by hand
man, how did they live
without books arriving
every day noon and night
when books are delivered
and words invade
and create
so many thoughts
to hold inside one's head

I go to bed
and there on the pillow
a book blocks my way
I reach for the lamp
on the nightstand
and knock over a stack of more books and more
they're chasing me
hazing me
facing me
testing me
taunting me
calling me
read me
no read me
no read me
I just scream
get out of my head
of my bed
of my house
off my stoop
STOP just STOP

what's in my head?
I don't know what ideas or thoughts are mine
anymore
there's jumble
in my brain
i'm in pain

and so
I swear off those brown paper packages
white labels and all
until one day
I will tell you all I have read
get it out of my head
and make room for more
until then
NO more. GO AWAY. Go away. go away.

Back To The Place

back to the place
i first saw your face
i came to say goodbye

back to the place
i first saw your face
i cannot say goodbye

make some space
let him go let him go
so there's room in your place
for newness and grace
that is what they say.

i'm back to the place
i first saw your face
they tell me to say goodbye
i want to say goodbye
i want to let you go
i want to show
myself and the world

that moving along
in life and in song
is the way of
today
so tomorrow could be filled
with joy

i'm back to the place
i first saw your face
and feel you fading away
i don't want you to stay
i don't want you to go
just cz they say so
you know

i'm back to the place
you first saw my face
and told me you wanted more
more is here
it's here it's here
but i'm back to the place
i first saw your face
and there's calm and peace
in place of need
to go back to the place
i first saw your face
I tell you it's all ok
maybe

there's joy and pain
together for now
until one leaves
and allows
joy to stay
pain to go
so until then
i'm back to the place
you first kissed my face

Chapter 5
Soul Quicksand

Pieces of Peace
Stronger in Places
He Sees Me
Don't Raise Your Voice
The One You Don't Want

Pieces of Peace

can there be peace
I think not
each human has got
a fingerprint
all their own
which shows
that we are all different
and not the same at all.
so how can there be peace
with the amount people
that are all different.
all.
i mean not even two people are alike,
never mind a husband and wife
or a group
or a town
or a country.

the Gods plunked us down here
all different
and we fight

for world peace
while the Gods throw their heads back
slap their knees
and laugh
and watch the show.
if they even have knees.

can there be peace
I think not
yet it seems to be
the goal in life
can't you see?
it's what the beauties
in the pageants want
world peace
and they are the best
of the best, right?
the prettiest of the pretties
the ones that climbed till the top
and they won't stop
until they announce
that their winning game
is to bring world peace
so they could win the sash.

have any of them brought about
world peace as of yet?
I think they forget

as soon as the crown sits
upon their head
and then they just wave at us.

can there be peace
I think not
accords have been drawn
by men of greatness
and typed up by
women
who are probably also great
accords between countries
at war
I forget why.
did we ever really know why?
I mean what is the real reason
countries
do not have peace with each other?
or is it like the sister and brother
fighting in the next room
and when their parent asks
what happened,
who started it?
they each tell a different story
and point fingers at one another
and then dad or mom says
make peace
anyway

who cares who started it
and why.
sister and brother pretend
to make peace
but they each still silently seethe
and think they were right
all along.
anyway.
and they start fighting again
when no one is looking.

can there be peace
I think not
what they and we call peace
is only a piece
of peace
to put out the flames
until everyone calms down
enough
just enough
so we can sleep at night
and then out come the elves
and night-owls
and do the thriller dance
together
and start a new fire
while everyone was calmly sleeping
and dreaming that the world was peaceful

and pleasant.

can there be peace
I think not.
there can be wishes of peace
thoughts of peace
plans for peace
hopes for peace
marches for peace
drummers for peace
dancers for peace
artists for peace
songs for peace
singers for peace
moms for peace
dads for peace
women and men and kids for peace
grandparents and aunts and uncles
for peace
signs for peace
stories of peace

so it's really all just
a journey for peace.
it's a journey people.
it's a journey.
piece by piece.
we have moments of peace

while we want it
and dream of it
and try in our own fingerprint way
to create it
and to bring peace.
each in our own way
together the world is filled
with many
pieces of peace.

Stronger in Places

i'm stronger in places
i don't wanna be strong
i want the Disney way
the easy way
the breezy cheesy princess way

i'm stronger in places
I don't wanna be strong
I climb and I try and I go for my dreams
I go for the guy, heart on the line
it worked for a while
it's magic for miles
and then
come the cracks
and like Alice I fall
wonderlands not wonderful
i'm broken and bruised
I sit and I cry and I try
to get back to where I was
my lips right on his
high on love and life

yet wonderland's dark
and bloody and bruised
i get up and fix up
the paces and spaces
grow strong once again
and off to the races of life
off to Disney
dreams and schemes
to make me believe
it all could be so
and it works for a while
we kiss and make up
my life straightens up
and yes we are stronger
go longer and farther
and more and more blessings
are strewn on our path
we smile and dance
Aladdin's lamp
life is good for a while
we smile and then
there's a crack...

i'm stronger in places
i don't wanna be strong
i want the Disney way
the easy way
the breezy cheesy princess way

He Sees Me

oh to be seen
for a second or two
he noticed and paused
and looked right through

oh to be seen
for a second or two
no words were passed
just a nod of the head
and then it was over
or so i thought

i was just seen
for a second or two
a screenshot was taken
my solemn look shaken
into a smile
that goes to the heart
the soul
and most of all

the memory
and fixes something broken.

i was just seen
for a second or two
nobody knew
but me
and he
and the two second snap
the pause
the frame
i see you
seeing me.

i was just seen
for a second or two
it's real
it happened
a moment not gone
or forgotten
until perhaps another
sees me
for a second or two
or more

i was just seen
for a second or two
did our eyes connect

does he know the effect
of me seeing him
see me
for a second or two?

Don't Raise Your Voice

don't raise your voice
my father would say
but he would raise his.
in the world of the man
the plan
was to keep us silent
smiling
while we followed the rules
his rules

don't raise your voice
my father would say
but he would raise his.
and so it was
do as I say
not as I do

don't raise your voice
my father would say
but he would raise his.
to keep us in line
the line he set

the be met
without question

don't raise your voice
my father would say
but he would raise his.
so I learned to use
my outside voice
inside me
on my mind, that denied
on my heart, that cried
on my soul, that yearned
to be heard
and my stomach
turned
with all the unspoken
with all the un-shouted
with all the silenced
with all the sounds
shut down to the ground
that humans need to make
or they shake
and quake
with fear
of the world

don't raise your voice
my father would say

but he would raise his
until one day
all the un-raised voices
of all the world
found each other
and
joined together
and staged a revolution
to find a solution
for a place and space
to award
the un-raised voices
their time in the sun
and once set free
the un-raised voices
spread like dandelion fluff
blown once
with closed eyes
and the seeds got planted
everywhere
never to be contained again.

and so
voices will be raised
whenever
wherever
however
forever

never to be silenced again
as long as dandelions shall live.

The One You Don't Want

when the one you don't want
wants you
what do you do
he calls and he sends
all the best
pretty things

but you don't want him
like he wants you

when the one you don't want
wants you
what do you do
you like the attention
the comments of love
you like to know someone
thinks you're above
all the other girls

but you don't want him
like he wants you

it's nice to know
that out in the world
out in the jungle
where animals tumble
and fight for survival
there's someone
that's fighting for you.

but you don't want him
like he wants you.

you're flattered and all
he thinks you're the one
and you are
but not for him.
you keep it a secret
so he won't get mad
and stop showing you
all of the tricks he can pull
the things he will do
when you just say i do

but you don't want him
like he wants you

you tire of swatting
his well meaning banter

his promises, jokes
and his plans forever after
for you
and him
to play in the world
when all you want
is the one who doesn't want you
like you want him

Chapter 6
Attention to Song

What if my Whole Life Was Wrong?
All I Can Do
It's A John Mayer Day
Stir the Pot Like Madonna

What if my Whole Life Was Wrong

i went to school
i followed the rules
what if my whole life was wrong

i played fair
i always shared
what if my whole life was wrong
anyway.

i toed the line
i stepped in time
what if my whole life was wrong

i helped the old lady
cross the street
i think my life was still wrong

i smiled at a child
i worked for a while
tired.
what if my whole life was wrong

i cried bitter tears
i regained my cheer
yet what if my whole life is wrong

i found inner peace
from the mountain and street
with teachers and preachers
and kiddies and aprons
yet still
my life seemed wrong

it was all ok
until one day
the music took me away.
and showed me my whole life was wrong.
how could one song
shake me and make me
see?

so i cried
and tried
to stop
in vain

i must follow along
to the keys and the song
it's been you all along
and now my whole life isn't wrong

All I Can Do

all i can do is hide
inside
my mind
and sigh

all i can do is stay
away
from all
today

all i can do
is beat
the drum
of time
that's gone

all i can do
is wait
and test
my faith

all i can do
is kick
and scream

all i can do
is watch
the world
keep on
keep on

all i can do
is think
of when
the music
played
and slowly
turn
it up
again

It's a John Mayer Day

when you fear and you tear
thru the world all around
when you stomp and you stamp
and slam and goddamn

when nothing goes right
and you fight with your brain
cz they all are a pain
all the people
you see
and hear
you just fear
that your dreams
will just die.

when you fear and you tear
thru the world all around
when you stomp and you stamp
and slam and goddamn

you want to feel good
as you should
as you could
because all is ok
for today
but you know that tomorrow
could bring war on the land
or war to just you and your kind
leaving some behind
that have one color God
and faith in the skin
that only some are in.

so what can you do
nothing.
but listen to John Mayer sing.
for a song or two maybe three
you know what will be will be
with fathers and daughters
and lovers and brothers
and mothers and sisters
and friendships and cities
and singers and drummers
will always live on
no matter what
there's always a song.
of John Mayer's.

Stir the Pot Like Madonna

Stir the pot
stir the pot
stir
stir stir the pot

like Madonna

whatcha gonna do
wear a mask and hide your face
ok ok so hide your face
but don't sit in place
but face
the other parts of you
your brain
your pain
your heart
your art
your stomp your stamp
your rage your cage
how you stirring
and showing you're caring

and daring
to change the status quo

Stir the pot
stir the pot
stir
stir stir the pot

like Madonna

don't just sit there
and let them rip Madonna apart
for blazing and razing
and changing and showing
herself her space
her place
her claim her stake
her owning the world she's in
come in
come on
break out break through
and do
something that will make everyone hate you
or love you
or ignore you
or wanna be you
don't just sit on your pot
stir it

Chapter 7
Compositions of Soul

I Am Where I Am
I Woke Up
Find Another You

I Am Where I Am

i am where i am
where i did not want to be
the light.
is for some.
not me.

i am where i am
where i did not want to be
the dark is free
where i could be you
you could be me.

i am where i am
where i did not want to be
mystery
hypocrisy
nighttime is daytime
June is July

yet waves of light
would not agree

or let me see the darkness
as glory.
so light came to greet me,
and set me free.
i am where i am
where i did not want to be
in flight thru the sky
on wings of faith
white and free.

taken and shaken
when battered and broken
against my will
to fulfill
my quest to see
the light
and where the bright
began

i am where i am
where i did not want to be I
could take you there.
with me.

I Woke Up

I woke up with a heavy heart
my head
could not part
with my pillow
my body heavy
on my bed
but still
my alarm insists
that it's time to rise
and shine
don't forget the shine part
it's important

I woke up with a heavy soul
I thought the morning
was supposed to be
a new start
a new chance
a new day
a clean slate

all those pretty things
waking up brings
but no

I woke up with a mixed up mind
the kind
that tells you it's all wrong
your life that is
and your life is you
so you're all wrong
you have been all along
all that striving
what a joke
only no one's laughing

I woke up with a list of things
to do
to go
to see
to be
only what nut job made that list
in a fit
of wanting to be perfect
well well I certainly don't feel like
ticking off
those things
I wrote down
that are making me hide

before the sun even chanced to rise
I mean it's 4 am

I woke up with a muddled head
so I sat up straight
to meditate
because that's what you're supposed to do
to start the day off well
to cast a spell
to call in God
and maybe if you're lucky
the Goddesses
and if you listen
you'll hear
what they want you to do
and then you get up and do it
goddamnit

So now what. what do I do
with this grown up person
that is me
that doesn't want to be
the one holding the world together
while being nice
and paying bills
and tucking my dreams
back into bed
while I get up and go

to the kitchen for coffee

suddenly
out of nowhere
the waves decide
it's time for the tide
to roll in
and take care of things
and wash away the mess
and address
what cannot be said
and so
I cry
and my head
falls back on my bed
with permission granted
to not want
what's in front of me
even the good things
and there are many good things
because i'm lucky

The tide that rolled in
also rolled out
leaving calm
and serene
feelings of clean
slates.

the day can begin
now that the seaweed
is gone from head
and the dread
is out with the sea
so I can do and be
anything
as long as I also do
some of the things
to keep the world from falling apart
at the seams

some of the things
not all of the things
so I can have time
to pluck
a teeny tiny thing
off of the list
of dreams
from the list
I pushed
under my pillow
and so the story goes
little by little
the world will see
that it can exist
relatively decently
without me

because i'm off
playing a song on the piano.

Find Another You

find another you?
i don't wanna
there are so many
fish in the sea
i don't want 'em

find another you?
i don't wanna
John Mayer said so
in his song
as he strums right along
let **him** find another you
so let him

i don't want a song
or a fish in the sea
i don't want to know
that New York City busses come and go
and there's always another
oh brother. oh sister.
Selena knows best

better than the rest
the heart wants what it wants.
i don't want another you
i'm not gonna find another you
another u will have to find me

bump into me at 6 am
on the train
in the diner
on a plane
getting coffee
messy hair in a bun
when i'm not looking
someone
someone
will have to find another
me

Chapter 8
Soliloquy

Waiting For What
Long Island Man
Gimme Some Rock n' Roll
Write Something Funny
Stairs to Nowhere

Waiting For What

how much of life is spent waiting.
so much.
what are we waiting for though
i mean, who knows about tomorrow.

how much of life is spent waiting.
too much.
who says it's too much?
maybe we could trust
that the wait
is really where it's at.

how much of life is spent waiting.
not much.
that is, if you think about it
and use it
that time spent waiting
to think your own thoughts
dream your own dreams
weave your own life
far away from reality.

maybe that's where reality is
in your own thoughts
in your own dreams
in your own plans
that you think
and create
with time you spend
waiting for something to happen
for someone to start
for them to get here
and meet you
and give you
and greet you
and treat you
to what it is
that you're waiting for.

waiting for coffee.
the green light
the children
to wake up
the sick one to heal
or to die.
or to try
to tell you the meaning of life
as they see it,
that you should not wait.

waiting,
thinking your thoughts
and planning your plans
and dreaming your dreams
and postponing death
and wishing for life
when you could just live
in this moment you're waiting.
and smile as you do
because no one can see
what you do while you're waiting.
you're creating.
life.
your life.

Long Island Man

have you heard about
Long Island man?
he tries to hide
he rides he dies
he rocks he rolls
and all the ladies love him.

have you heard about
Long Island man?
he prays he strays
he spends his days
kissing and dissing
and all the ladies love him.

have you heard about
Long Island man?
he hides behind
his magic inside
illusions and tricks of his choosing.
and all the ladies love him

have you heard about
Long Island man?
who's shading and fading
and playing and graying
yet still. He's hot as coal.
and tells the ladies
whatever they need to hear.
so there.
and they all think they love him.

have you heard about
Long Island man?
no?
who?
where?
hmmmm
I haven't seen
or heard from Long Island man.
where and what is Long Island man?
i don't know.
do you?
I forgot.
Did he exist?

Gimme Some Rock n' Roll

gimme some rock
gimme some roll
woweee
Sir Bowee
get me out
from the pressure
i'm under
and
he gets me
owwwwt.

gimme some rock
gimme some roll
where's the Mercury
the killer
the queen
he's dead
but not his fat
bottom
girls!
they're alive

and kikin' at the show
so you know
you Bohemians!
the drums must go on
and I must be there
to vibrate
and gyrate
be obscene
where it's cool
to be free
ultimately
that's what we all want, right?

gimme some rock
gimme some roll
roll me with the stones
satisfy me
defy me
blast and blare
I don't care
I want it now I want it loud

Purple Rain me
Prince me
convince me
that there's music playing
somewhere
in the world

or it's dangerous.
precarious.
do you think
i'll stay alive
without it?
doubt it.

so Floyd, you wanna tell
heaven from hell?
so go.
leave it all behind
and follow the King
of
Pop
to a place
where no one cares
about fears and stares
and dumb things
and job things
follow the King
that leads the way
to the rock
to the roll
that's the only thing
that could delete
the pain
of life as it is
from your brain

or go.
completely.
utterly.
insane.

gimme some rock
gimme some roll
they didn't text back
or call you?
ha.
who would be there to know?
not me.
i'm with the rock
i'm with the rowwwwwwl
ahhh.
delete
delete
delete.
you're canceled.
for now.
i mean why'd u only call me
when your'e high,
anyway?
now i'm the high one
high on the music
high on the rock
high on the roll.
whose happy now?

gimme some rock
gimme some roll
Joan Jett
make me wet
you bet
i'm coming
home
with new beats
in my soul
and my hole
world
will forever be invaded
cascaded
serenaded
by the sound
of the music
in the air
everywhere
everyone
that was there
is a part of me now
magical people.
anyhow
it's all about the music
or it's nothing.
nothing at all
either - or.

the rest is filler
filler I tell you.
I know.
for sure.

so gimme some rock
and gimme some roll
how funny
i'm happy
at last
for a moment in time
when i'm with the the rock
and i'm with the roll.
anyway
it's all about
when the music
plays.
and then
well, it's just whatever.

Write Something Funny

write something funny
she says
after reading my stories
of pain and regret

write something happy
she says
your life is so sad
you could do what I do
I just put pink icing
on everything
and then it's a-ok!

write something new
she says
and then rip out the
sad poems
and replace them with glad

write something light

and bright
not about the darkness
of your night
that's why we sleep at night
when it's dark
so we can pretend
the night does not
exist
for us, anyway
like when a kid hides
behind a lamppost
and his eyes are closed
so he thinks no one
can see him
if he cant see them.

write something cheerful
so that we smile
oh, I know. like when Dad used to tell me
to smile while I washed the dishes
clean the floors
and took care of his kids
because he married someone (mom)
that could not, would not, and did not
do it (i mean beauty queens don't do those things)

wipe that frown off your teenage face
and do it with grace

and smile
while you're at it

so I used to smile
while I was at it.

write something for me
you see
I cannot read
how painful
your life is and was
for then I may need to believe
that it's not ok
to smile thru the tears
and fears
and events that come
that teach us things
that are mirrors for us
that make us beat pillows with baseball bats
in classes we take
to erase
the pain
of yesterday

write something happy, I say?
okay. I will.
after you face your pain.
so when will that be, I ask.

pain? what pain? there is no pain.
only rainbows, says she
now write happy things for me!

and so.
I will write something happy.
what's happy?
clowns.
I will write about clowns.
but wait. i'm scared of clowns.

Stairs to Nowhere

sometimes
you need to find
the stairs to nowhere
to climb, to hide
to end up nowhere.

sometimes
you need to find
the place you're lost inside
it's only found
on the stairs
to nowhere.

sometimes
you need to find
what's really on your mind
the kind of thoughts that take you
on the spiral stairs
to nowhere.

and you end up where you started

wound up,
wound down,
erased and chased
by thoughts you found
on the stairs
to nowhere.

where can you go
to seek, to show
the world you know
that you're on the stairs
to somewhere
the stairs
that lead to nowhere.

you go you flow
you row you tow
you sleep
you wake
you chase
you take
the roads that lead to nowhere.

it's time to find
the up-way climb
that tires your mind
your body your soul
it's up up up

one step to trek
and then another
then you find
your peace of mind
up high
on the climb
on the stairs
that lead to nowhere.

come down around
and shine
and find
what's found on the climb
inside
you.

About the Author

Find out when volume 2 is out here:
http://estherfink.com/book-2/

Esther Litchfield-Fink is an award-winning writer andmarketing consultant from New York City.

For a complete portfolio of writing awards and publications

visit estherfink.com
contact: info@litchfieldstrategies.com

www.ingramcontent.com/pod-product-compliance
Lightning Source LLC
Chambersburg PA
CBHW041823090426
42811CB00010B/1094